THE FRIGHTENERS

THE

FRIGHTENERS

Sean O'Brien

ISBN: 1 85224 013 X

First published 1987 by
Bloodaxe Books Ltd,
P.O. Box 1SN,
Newcastle upon Tyne NE99 1SN.

Bloodaxe Books Ltd acknowledges
the financial assistance of Northern Arts.

Typesetting by Bryan Williamson, Manchester.

Printed in Great Britain by
Tyneside Free Press Workshop Ltd, Newcastle upon Tyne.

For My Mother

Acknowledgements

Acknowledgements are due to the following publications in which some of these poems first appeared: *Bête Noire, Encounter, The Honest Ulsterman, The Literary Review, London Magazine, North, The Observer, Poetry Review, Slightly Soiled, Strawberry Fare, The Times Literary Supplement*, and *Verse*.

Contents

IN A MILITARY ARCHIVE

In a Military Archive

The mirror on this corridor
Detains them in its waiting-room.
Sporadically the backward clock
Remembers its authentic boom
And flings the dead men to their knees.
They rise. They smoke. They watch their hands.
They mend the furniture and read.
The King's Own ----shire Ampersands,
Preserved as footnotes in the texts
Of Hockley, Blunden, Hart et al.,
At ease in the grave-geographies
Of Arras, Albert and Thiepval.
Now literature is sent, as once
Were razor-blades and letters,
That the dead may study suffering
In the language of their betters.

The Dampers

Damp weather wrings its yellow hands,
Staining the lungs as it fingers for lesions.
It's here, with a velvety flourish,
Liver-spotted pillowslips. Now leather smudges,
Jackets wear the badge of dissolution,
Rooms burst sickly into flower.
The bubbling voices of radio liars
Drift on drowning frequencies.
Damp nineteenth century music parts
The cardboard necks of violins.
Damp literature, damp diaries,
Damp biscuits, damp regression:
At home, in the damp stacks of *Tiger* and *Wizard*,
With four-colour heroes whose red, white and blue
Has survived on your lack of belief.
Roy of the Rovers? The Wolf of Kabul?
They have sunk through the page and congealed
On the air-raid shelter's floor
In an adipose mixture of ink and ambition,
The ultimate mimetic act.
Why, even the coffins are damp
On their blocks at the makers, awaiting,
As midnight approaches with revels and vows,
Those punters whom the damp detains.
Goodbye. There are more missing faces
Condensing the wrong sides of mirrors,
Or staring back blankly from photos
And shell-holes, still mouthing their names
In the silt of all cancelled intentions.
To drain from the outline and vanish:
You melt, when the offer is made.

Young Howard

Two aunts in garish rosy prints
Sat waiting in the head man's room,
Intent on their vocation; there
'To take me home'. They called me in
From cricket to my life, my life.

They worked in shifts. I dreamed
They stroked my arm until it bled.
Their eyes reflected me alone
With the trust fund of grief I have
Never been able to manage myself.

Today the rear window flashes
Summons to its madman, me.
I'm better now. I know they'd say
*It's best indoors. It's getting cold
And no one wants to see you there.*

Born just postwar, I live there still,
Young Howard with his special pain,
Largactil crust across his mouth.
I watch the dead in photographs.
My drunken flier with his charm,

My drunken blonde with her estate,
Both shovelled off the road in bits
Along with the MG, kept me
In shorts between the knees of aunts
Equipped with love, with metal combs.

I'm sick of all my annuals,
But every Sunday as I count
Each piece of gravel on those graves
I live my life. I stand erect.
They tell me I am feeling proud.

A Master

For half my life I tried to learn from you.
You gave me cities, voices, other books
And space to make what might at last be mine.
I know now I won't match what you can do:
Who else could show how disappointment looks
When honestly persuaded into line?

The Realists

The rows. Remorse. The birthday guilt
It seemed we'd always waited for. — *waiting to grow up.*
How quickly childhood makes itself
The subject of all pain. At least
Unhappiness was made to match. ?

We can talk of the fear on the landing,
Empty shops and lightless Sundays,
Bare legs and cold knuckles. The voices
Transmitted their coded distress
From room to room, half-audibly.

Conspirators in adult hurt,
We were given an atlas to look at.
The globe like a clockface described
Its true circle and all the routes
Guided us back to this room

Where we share an impoverished tongue –
What's wise, what's best, what shan't be thought
By persons whose business is penance
For lives that were never begun.
This evening is an afterlife:

Looking and carefully looking away
We rehearse the responsible half-truths
Like adults, with habits of fiction.
The words will be all we can make,
So that meaning deserts them, then self,

Until only the voices are left
For the listeners awake on the stairs,
Who have learned to believe this is how
These affairs are conducted, and think
Of a day they will speak for themselves.

Civilians

After eating with friends, after music and wine,
The citizens lay down. Some dreamed
Of subways to the oven's mouth.
All took their passports to the flames.

In the cellar's cellar
People wrote journals. The pardons
Awarded to God were so many.
Now we own the manuscripts.

Brave to have needed a coat,
To have paused in the hall at the mirror,
To brush away dandruff,
To check for a pen.

Be lyrical and serious, they say,
And try to think of history as home.

Genius Loci

Think what virtue you have squandered
On technique, you foolish boy.
The good die young but are never
Found wanting or writing in places like this.

This evening you dine at the Turd Café.
No smoking, no toilets,
No tenpenny pieces, but doughnuts
Bleeding resignedly into your hand.
If it's penance you want, go and squat
By the seawall and hear the fish fart
In wet darkness from Dymchurch to Câp Finisterre.

Remember that autoerotically
Damp gazetteer in the redblooded atlas
The empire bequeathed you to play with?
This too is entered. Now ask for a match.
Your face and my arse, says the serving-hatch.

The Era

The era we are entering,
You and I, our shrugging grocer
And the listener in the wall,
Won't feel the lack of history.
There'll be the dripping overflow
On green-brocaded brick,
The sound of nothing going on.
We'll be waiting for muffled reports
From a neighbouring district,
But if they should come
We'll do nothing:
The last of our talents
Survives in good order
The vanishing language,
While amnesia declassifies
The smoke that swarms across the roofs.
If I try out a gesture,
A former caress, you'll neither
Answer nor resist, but lie
With a unique indifference,
While in the streets the searchers go
From door to door
Holding the death-lists
And asking the victims
To find their own names.

Summertime
(for Richard Richardson, Kent NUM)

The news is old. A picket line
Is charged and clubbed by mounted police.
Regrettable. Necessity.
You have to take a balanced view.
That kind of thing can't happen here
And when it does it isn't true.

Adore yourself and in the body's
Shrivelled province bask and breed.
Indulge your fudged affairs and lust
For what your terror says you need.
It's hot. Lie down and vegetate.
There are no politics, no state.

At noon on Brighton beach it's clear
Why heatwaves make the English glad.
Beneath that burnt imperative
In oiled, obedient ranks they lie,
To forge a beachhead close to home
And found the final colony.

You have to take a balanced view.
That kind of thing can't happen here,
And when it does it isn't true.

The Red Hospital

(for Steve Johnston)

The train stopped this evening. I looked
And the place still had flames in the windows.
I knew what they meant about cold.
The Victorians wanted a hospital
Bigger, more "moving" than death,
As elaborate as empire, as law.
It unmarried the poor, since it could,
And they came out in boxes.
It stood at the street-end, a red-brick
Cathedral of cold, like a court or a jail,
And the terrace was cold, in its mock-Gothic shade.
I could feel it by thinking *red hospital*,
Watching the clock to learn by heart
The tables of its endless afternoons,
While grandmother slept and the fire
Decayed to red rubble. The phrase was stuck
Like dirty language in my mouth –
Red hospital, like *fuck* and *cunt*
Repeating themselves on the walls.
The cold came through the door by right.
The only good was punishment.
But the old men were angels, or almost –
My grandmother said – in blankets
On balconies, nearer reward or relief,
And because they were counting the hours
Were free of their sins. They could die.
It's thirty years on. The wards are shut,
The terraces ash and the workhouse
A word you explain. My grandmother's
Vanished with empire and sin, and there's only
This place between places, made over
To carparks and lights. But it's home.
I can tell, when I loyally shiver,
Go over my tables and swear.

The Allotment

The cold eases over my wrists. I'm at home
With the details, at dusk in October.
My Grandad's allotment's an ashtray
Crammed with herbal cigarettes. The red coals
Fade in the cucumber frames and there's sure
To be frost in the brazier by morning.
Around us the other old men on their plots
Have knocked off for a smoke before home.
They wear their breath in grey balloons
And have fireproof hands and no lungs.
I should mention the moon with milled edges,
The roar down the tunnel of air
That means somebody's scored. But I can't.
I'm the future, a gaberdined dwarf
In the cap of the privileged school
You could see past the willows and sidings.
The spire denoted Victorian money
And officers honoured on plaques,
The names that had employed the men
I stood among. They did not mention this
Or speak to me at all, but went on
Coughing expertly and waiting. I should say
What's not true, that I saw how the ice
Would step into the footprints they left
On the cinders while saying goodnight.
I should find an impersonal manner
To dignify Garbutt and Doonan and Briggs,
The wide-suited utility scarecrows,
War-veterans all, who said nothing
Of what they had been, but persisted
In tending their plots and choking to death,
Which was none of my business
But comes back this evening as guilt,
Then as anger, to stiffen my hand
While I write, to remain when the poem
Refuses to end or forgive, when the cold
Has come home and the old men are waiting.

Trespass

The downlands, private under drizzle,
Hoard their woodcut oaks for those
Who own them, who are England.
Horse-commanding wheat-haired daughters
Natter down the gated lanes
Beneath a roof of hawthorns.
Mist admits them, phantom *politesse*.
You take the smugglers' road beneath the fields,
Dead ground without the government,
And as you travel, wonder
What conspiracy this is
That needs a mask of leaves and rain
To find its right of way, and how
You know this hidden route so well.

Song of the South

We change our cars and eat our meat.
There are no negroes on our street.
Our sons are sailing with the fleet.
We keep our mania discreet.

We take our secretaries on trips.
We have a taste for furs and whips.
We look to Panama for ships.
It hurts us when the market slips.

We place our cash in Krugerrands.
We rule the waves, so say the bands
At Brighton, where we own the sands.
You won't find blood upon our hands.

Conservative in politics,
We have no time for lefty pricks
Who sympathise with wogs and spicks.
We print the kind of shit that sticks.

We even bought a moralist.
We fund his comic, keep him pissed.
Just now we need him to exist,
The sweaty little onanist.

It is of property we dream.
We like to think we are a team.
We think that poverty's a scream.
We're still more vicious than we seem.

And speaking of the next world war,
The bang we've all been waiting for,
We will survive: We are the law
That shuts and locks the shelter door.

Unregistered

Six cranes where Baltic vessels come
As if home to the flatness of the land
Which is only not water by virtue
Of no one agreeing to drown.

Six cranes for which nowhere
Is far too precise, with low sheds
And the minimum bollards
And seemingly nobody there.

Six cranes where the ballet is off
And no one jumps ship.
That's the street, that's the pub
And the poster of Showaddywaddy.

Six cranes where Baltic vessels come
With coal to break the strike.
Does Mr Scargill think me think
The revolution starts like this?

Souvenirs
(for Ken Smith)

The early men play pool for drink.
The wind jumps like a dog at the door
And the waiting begins and begins.

This isn't the drunk between ships:
Now the schedules are yellow, known only
To locked wards' memorious headers

Reciting the last of the facts they could bear.
The punters play or watch the rest
And polish halves like souvenirs,

And nobody talks because decency means
It's too soon and too late for their stories again.
In Baltic Chambers, open to the sky,

Are a telephone book
And a jar of salt herring,
And out off the jetty's a matchless collection

Of tin cans and corpses
And things rotted out of their names
In the slack water after the tide.

Now it won't cost a penny
To go down and touch it,
To read your black palm for yourself,
If you can, now the lines have all vanished.

Terra Nova

In late afternoon, when the snow began,
The sirens of craft on the river,
Bound outwards from elsewhere to elsewhere,
Reminded the city of sailings –
North Cape, the Baltic forests, Arkangelsk.
No lines of mileage link us now.

And the footprints all over the shoreline
Were only historians, out
For a blow in the shipping museum.
Trespassers who do not drown
Will suffer prosecution, said a sign
On the dockside. No pleasuring now,

No stink and no electric suits,
Just De La Pole coated in white,
Facing inland, his arms by his sides,
Like a man among men in the queue
For the card, for the insult called
History, that won't pay the rent.

The snow fell, like the waste of a subject.
It fell on grids of terraces,
Abandoned quays and stray containers,
On boarded-up windows, in doorways,
In tenfoots, on flame-blackened landings,
Steadily out of the burnt-orange night.

It fell on the tracks behind houses,
On sheds in the vandalised goodsyards,
On scrub and the river and even
The decks of the sea-going shipping,
Which left us the one consolation
Of knowing it snows on them too.

Then I wished the whole place would embark,
The schools and mills and hospitals and pubs
In a team of all talents, a city of lights
Singing *Sod you old England, we're leaving*
For work, heading out on a snow-boat
To sail off the compass for home.

Initiative

In folds of heathland patched with scrub
There are serious nutters at large.
You have seen them, perhaps, from your car.

They are rained-on, unsubsidised creatures
Long out of the fashion (some shoeless,
Some nude) with those comedy accents

The services used to be good at.
Their present is nobody's business,
So don't talk to them about nippers

Or fires in buckets, or windfalls:
They go for your throat not your poems.
They're losers. They fell from employment

(Assuming they had it), and cities,
And shedding ambition (assuming they had it)
Along with their names, dribbled south

Until blocked by the sea. Now they squat
In their shit and are none too appealing.
The fact is they're weak, and they think

This is something we've done, and they're right.
So their good days are brain-deaths of waiting,
Their bad ones are dining off cardboard,

And whom do they hurt but themselves?
But it has to be said: they're polluting
A landscape they've not even paid for

And haven't the wit to develop.
Besides, our ecologists tell us
Their footsteps are deadly to ants,

That the nightingale flees from the stench
And the rare little bustard is threatened
Wherever they breathe.
                    Yes, of course,

But our hands have been tied. It's the law.
And so all we can do now is wait.
Let us hope, as the summer goes out,

That with stimuli – cold and short rations,
The corpses beside them at dawn –
They will learn to eat soil, and to burrow,

To go where the privacy is, to dispose
Of themselves where our methods have failed.
Should they succeed and the JCBs

Roll up to plug the little holes,
We shall, of course, erect a plaque,
To prove our faith in enterprise.

London Road

As I walked out on London Road
Towards the close of day,
I grew confused, and it appeared
I must have lost my way,

For when I stopped and looked around
The hills of Housman's blue
Had ceased to be a colour
And became a point of view.

It matched the spanking outfits
Of the cops who blocked the road.
The only things they seemed to lack
Were bucketfuls of woad.

One said, 'Now son, what business
Takes you out beyond the pale?
Are you quite sure you're what you seem,
A blue Caucasian male?

'You wouldn't be a picket
Or a dike from CND?
We've orders from her Majesty
To round them up, you see.'

'I'm going down the pub,' I said,
'Like every Friday night.
If it's OK with you, I'd like
To exercise that right.'

Apparently this angered him:
He took me by the balls.
His breath was acrid in my face,
Like bullet-holes in walls.

'We're here tonight rehearsing
For insurgencies ahead,
And if you breathe a bloody word
We'll beat you nine parts dead.

'We'll ask the questions afterwards
And charge you for the mess.
There'll also be a list of crimes –
You'll find that you confess.

'There'll be no point in asking
For the date of your release:
These days we throw away the key
When folks disturb the police.

'Take our advice: get off the street.
Stay in and watch TV.
Unless the law is absolute
The people can't be free.'

I turned and passed a barrier
In fear of an attack.
It isn't safe on London Road
And I'm not going back,

For in that land of lost content
Where facts are redefined
I've seen the enemy within,
The ones I left behind,

And as I walked I heard a song
Stage-whispered on the air,
Subversive in its sentiment,
The sound of no one there:

You poets of the little songs
Devoted to the muse –
You shouldn't be surprised, my lads,
To find you sing the blues.

The Mechanical Toy Museum

In the mechanical toy museum
At the end of Brighton's Palace Pier
Ten new pence will buy five old,
For history suffers inflation as well

And Jean Boudin might not believe
How big the smudged brown coins appear,
Designed to fit a pauper's eyes
Or the Jolly Nigger's thrifty tongue.

But no one is short of a penny in here
And that crimson-lipped, liquorice
Cast-iron slave is not one of the relics
Preserved in this tomb of Amusements.

Take care. These are delicate engines.
The pin-table predates the tilt,
Two threadbare teams stand riveted
In goalless extra time and the girls

In the peepshow must never be still
Or their bones will step out of their skins.
It keeps you fingering your change,
This taste for proofs of entropy.

Best of all, watch the beheading.
'Madame Guillotine est morte,'
A visitor carefully tells his son,
Who is keen to observe the procedure again.

But when the Bastille springs open,
Why, every time, does it seem that the corpse
Will pluck the straws from his spouting neck,
Take up his perruked head and walk

With absolute confidence back
Down the mad-mirrored ormolu halls
Of the *ancien regime*, as if we had
Never existed, still less eaten cake?

RYAN

Ryan is a misplaced person, a liar who means what he says. He insists he's a conscience but shows none himself.

His first remarks were like interference from a foreign station and seemed wholly private. At an early stage he showed an appetite for the experience of others, whether they liked it or not. He gave it his name, convinced that otherwise it would mean nothing.

He has access to information I've not got. Conversely he has no idea at all of how to behave round here. If you met him in a pub you would regret it – but you'd do it again. Anyway, what do you mean by going in that sort of pub?

He is always leaving or has just gone: only in a backward glance is he wholly himself. He was born expecting something quite different. His response to disappointment is rancour: he wants to know more than the people he blames. His dignity would sink this island if he let it all out at once. If you think he's insufferable you're probably right: but if you *say* so I'll send him round to your house.

How Ryan Got His Start in Life

The clank of supernatural machinery
Awoke me. So this was the life.
There were galleries, catwalks,
Stopcocks and sumps. There were beam-engines
Sinking and rising and sliding
In coats of gold oil, like a theory
Made fact and abandoned to beauty,
To prove itself over and over to no one.
A roof, I proposed, was obscured by the steam
Which was all these endeavours produced.
Some small high panes shed snowy light.
I left, down humming lanes of plant,
Stepping out on a street near the river
I still haven't seen, by a half-silted dock
That was swallowing snow without let.
A gull came gliding through the flakes
And then posed on a bollard. Was this
A bureaucrat? It worried me,
This life without a form to fill.
A clock on a black church said morning –
I looked for a drink and am doing it now,
At this bar where the eggs have been pickled
As long as the taciturn punters,
While afternoon drains out of lunchtime.
My liver is damaged already. I write this
In Stingo on blood-red formica,
And wish you were here, whoever you are.

Ryan at Home

Contraceptives crisp with frost
And turds gift-wrapped in yellow pages,
The glamour-girls' *membra disiecta*
Shedding their gloss with their papery skins –
They lie, as if only a moment ago
The monsters' working lunch dispersed
At the terrible news: this is home.
It's Saint Crapula's Square
And the knee-trembling district,
Whose sensitives want to be Rimbaud
Or Hitler, where sound drains away
Through a grille to the sewers
And all the Victorians said
About wanking turns out to be true.
Sweet home: the slab of sluiced grey hearts
And the church with its sensible hours.
The maps are discreet and the texts
Where a marginal reference is scented
Are shelved in a library not even the Pope
Could unlock nor a Frenchman imagine.
A town without transport or drink,
Where the papers are vetted
Of all but the innocent a's and the's
Like stammering youths in a chemist's.
Though counsel dutifully phone
Locked offices where flies are wintering,
The torturers keep to their punishing schedules.
The screams of the random arrested
Are stretched beyond all recognition.
Their answers could only be wrong.
Eccles or Eichmann or Ryan himself,
Everyone has to be somewhere,
And this is the place I was thought of,
My mission to hand out the shits
By declaring it Sunday forever.

Ryan's Vocation

(for Steve Knowles)

The yellow lamps hang underneath the smoke,
Expensive moths that should be somewhere else,
Discreetly overlooking the affairs
Of those with style and more than one address.
They worry us. We're torpid devotees
Of Scampi Crunch and torn and worried mats
Inscribed with inkless biros by the daft.
Those fittings nag our long bad faith
By promising elsewhere. Our articles
Are habit, disappointment, anomie,
A taste for muddy beers and pubs like this,
Whose tedium we've trained to share with all
Like-minded punters disinclined to speech.
There are no names, no other lives in here,
No talents or good ways of killing time.
What links us is the way we sit and brood
On all what little happens cannot mean,
Like revolution, money or free Bells.
The landlord polishes away the light
Along the bar, then gives it back and stands
Remembering the faces it contains,
As if they'd had the sense to up and go
And weren't observing him observing them,
The ornamental critics of his style,
His clothmanship, short measures and the ban
He hopes to universalise one day.
And we for our part labour to achieve
Paralysis, to save us going home,
Aspiring to the stillness of our gods –
The toucan doomed to reproduce our thirst
Forever with a dry glass at his beak,
The girl from Babycham who promises
That sex was good in nineteen fifty-eight.
Tonight, dear gods, may I donate my tongue
For polishing, to join you on the shelf,
To wear the speechless look of long disuse
And sit among your sacred cack, the plates
From Lowestoft, the green glass cat, the Queen,

That paraplegic octopus, those caps
Whose frigates' names outlive their crews. Let me
Give up the ghost of all action and stay.
Let traffic shudder me, time dust me down
To perfect disregard, a curio
No one would steal or even care to break.

Ryan's Rebirth

I step from the wardrobe unblinking.
My coat wears the contours of sleep
And my mouth has been pissed in by goats,
But otherwise I am unchanged,
Unaged, unloved, unspeakably myself.
The names and rooms are new,
Like the speed at which damage approaches
To offer its tongue to your mouth.
I am hired to suffer, you tell me,
To remake your language, erotic routine
For when love has a stammer; to offer
My dick in good faith to the night
And the outcry inside it; play
With pillowed hair and find
A handkerchief for pain – all this on behalf
Of the cackhanded god of my metre,
And I in return am unburdened by feeling.
I love it. I love it to death when the leaves
In the calendar fret for a crisis –
Those phone calls and notes, getting hard
During meetings, not catching the eye
Of the other whose clothes will be mixed
With your own in the morning; the effort
Of marriage, in which case the penis
Goes home like a coward for money,
In which case its agent gets up for the papers
With one girl asleep and the other on pills
And enquires too late if this shuddery complex
Of adult emotion and juvenile crime
Is not after all less seductive than boredom
And merely a means of election to pain –
But the whole transformation from lovers to clients
Is simply a process that needed to happen,
Which none of those lyric perfections
With her under trees and her hand down your pants
Can arrest at this date or at any to come.
I am your creature and I know the answers
You want but would rather not bear to be told.
Now I sit at your desk and transcribe the grey details

Exactly in agony's order and know
For the length of this business I'm back in the world –
And if in the midst of the labour I tell you
A job that's worth doing's worth doing forever,
Then that is my nature, which does not exist,
Except when you went me: so make up your mind –
There is work to be done while you ponder on that.

Ryan and the Life to Come

There's ground you cannot farm or build on.
It's found after sidings and prefabs,
All tussocks and halfbricks, with sheds
Like the bases of doomed expeditions.

Left to myself I should gravitate there,
At home like the madman of Hessle,
With his orange-box encampment
As lavish with signs as an airbase –

No sneakers no creepers no polices
In ten-foot high letters to advertise fear.
Woken at dawn by my bubbling chest,
With the fog close up and the river

A funeral *tong* from the lightship,
Perhaps I would come to consider the rest
As an indolent meantime, a waste
Of the chance to know nothing, claim all

And to speak my own trivial language –
Its jabbered ellipses and sly repetitions,
Unbreakable meaningless code.
And then I suppose I would die,

Gone out like a sheep by the hedgerow,
My fame the discomfiting feeling
Of aimless appraisal, politely endured
By any unfortunate visitor there.

The gods are not perfect. They hate us.
I might have to be one myself.
If so, make it earthy, a no-name,
And mindless and truthful as well.

Ryan in Winter

To be homeless took only a second:
The big house was back out of sight
And here I was, covered in somebody's snow
Like a man made a fool on a beach,
While the yew trees discreetly shed
Handfuls of flakes like a word to the wise
Meaning *Leave before anything happens.*
You don't want a scene or the law.

But that wasn't an option. I reached
For the flask of pure spirit
I hoped was in one of the pockets,
Then made for the pond in the roses
And looked for my face
In its cloudy steel mirror.
It came up to meet me, impatiently staring.
I asked, 'Are you certain you're mine?'

And the air seemed to crack like a glasshouse
As if with this modest enquiry
I'd fractured a general truth. So before
I'd been awkward. Now that was a comfort.
I quartered the lawn for an hour,
Remembering sums and my Latin
And hoping my name would survive.
When I looked at my footprints I saw
I'd completed a phrase with a flourish:
It told me that Ryan was here.

But then, so were *they*, more of the bastards
To hand on their misery lessons.
They were moving through the house
As though their time were occupied,
Fingering objects – this hardback, this snowstorm,
This jumper, this bucket of prawns
That they couldn't explain having bought.
When they weren't doing that
They were watching the lawn and then waiting.
For what? For the trees to say thank you?

Thank you for making a place where before
There was nothing but us?

If only wicked people polish books
Then only mad ones fuck their safes.
I too was intrigued to discover
How this was accomplished. I'd thought
It required a massive square prick
(UnEnglish idea) but in fact
There's a good deal of pain
And the use of the hinges.

Afterwards he sat and smoked,
Remembering he couldn't read.
She sat and understood him for a bit.
They talked about the snow like property.
Expensive children came and pissed them off.
And that was that – and like a fool
I'd thought something would happen.
Perhaps they'd been murdered already –
How else to account for their thinness of texture?
How else to account for the glow on the skyline
That smells like a city ablaze?
I'm leaving you this in the shed
And imagine you'll know what to do,
Which is more than I'd claim for myself,
So I've gone into town for a warm.

Ryan's Farewell

Tonight the summer opened like a park
Seen distantly, a blue-green reservation,
Lamps flicked on among the woods,
On lake and lawn. RSVP.
The moon hung like a furnace-mouth
Where all the names of heaven burned
A lengthy correspondence with your kind –
Or I'd gone past believing that sense
Could be decently made of the place,
But I had a last look at the details.
Luminous cricketers quit the pitch
Like heroes blessed by radium.
In afterlight the rhododendrons
Shed themselves and lime-trees twitched
Like mummers with too many lank green hands.
Beer seethed in jugs. Beside the road
The drowned man in his standing pool
Turned over and his shoulder whitely tore
The cloth-of-green that heat and rot had woven.
The clawfooted beeches furnished the woods
To a nursery's comforting scale,
Like the cretin-sized "A" meaning Abergavenny
Engraved in the gamekeeper's lintel.
So much to announce the mere self
With its dim little claims on tradition,
To land given shape by possession, by charm,
By the snivel of chords from the organ,
Entwining the bellrope and fading
But never entirely meaning to go.
These people would tear out your eyes
And buy gifts for their mothers, then bore you
With both as they stood the next round.
I'd failed. I was free to abandon this life
Without once understanding the facts
That could never be trusted or altered,
Or grasping what "sensible" meant.
On the hilltop I listened: the ocean
Unpicking, restitching its border. Not there.

And the keyhole of light on the forest was someone
Believing they'd made me already. Not there.
I would step through myself like a mirror,
To enter the index of air and have done.

Envoi

Or else on a road between roads in warm darkness
Corruption was waiting, a drench of cut roses
Left out in a guileless tin bucket –

A tremor of pastoral weakness
For things in themselves,
Meaning sex, meaning state, meaning here –

And that was me finished, believe it,
Caught out with my pants down in Sussex,
Bone-thirsty and craving for skin.

The chestnut's candlepower lights me home.
Another wife is waiting in her house
With strong tea and clean sheets and my new name

Tucked into her cleavage. The police
Are just putting the drunkards to bed,
Having mastered their nicknames. The ocean

Is crooning at Brighton and if you say money
It's something we'll have to regret
And make do with. Believe me. I'll promise

It's just until morning, I'll tell you
Tonight I could almost believe it myself,
But do not be misled by these tenses:

Suppose I agree to this pleasure: remember
I'm nowhere near finished with you,
So expect me, be sleepless and listen
For what I might mean when I stop.

KINGDOM OF KIEV

After This Poem

After this poem, perhaps it is evening.
Perhaps I am pleasantly tired?
More likely I'm knackered. Perhaps
The near ocean resuming its sound
Like the endless unzipping of silk
Will incite me to bed, or perhaps
I will feel like a drink: but in fact
It is simply a walk I require –
A mile down streets the effort seems
To have rinsed of its language for once,
To replace it with breathable air.
Across cool mats of sodium
Spread by the streetlights, I drift
Past benches upholstered with shadow,
The drivers asleep in their whispering cabs
And the girls who are tired from dancing,
Who lean under trees holding shoes,
And I find I am glad when the facts
Can be empty of all but themselves:
Which is when I remember the others.
Indoors and unlucky this evening
They shout at the walls through the smoke
As the paper goes blank on their desks.
Some have given up, and staring out
Could see me as I pause below,
A character the yawning moon
Declines to animate tonight,
While others burn the dictionary and drink,
And the rest persevere through a dead-shift
Attended by coffee and heartburn,
Afraid after all they have nothing to say,
Afraid that tautology rules, O.K.
They'd never believe it if I
Were to affer this alingual walk
As a proof that the thing will emerge,
The mad cousin of what they imagined,
Imperfect, but able to tell you its name
And blessed, it appears, with a personal cry.
They'd never believe it. Me neither.

46

Cousin Coat

You are my secret coat. You're never dry.
You wear the weight and stink of black canals.
Malodorous companion, we know why
It's taken me so long to see we're pals,
To learn why my acquaintance never sniff
Or send me notes to say I stink of stiff.

But you don't talk, historical bespoke.
You must be worn, be intimate as skin,
And though I never lived what you invoke,
At birth I was already buttoned in.
Your clammy itch became my atmosphere,
An air made half of anger, half of fear.

And what you are is what I tried to shed
In libraries with Donne and Henry James.
You're here to bear a message from the dead
Whose history's dishonoured with their names.
You mean the North, the poor, and troopers sent
To shoot down those who showed their discontent.

No comfort there for comfy meliorists
Grown weepy over Jarrow photographs.
No comfort when the poor the state enlists
Parade before their fathers' cenotaphs.
No comfort when the strikers all go back
To see which twenty thousand get the sack.

Be with me when they cauterise the facts.
Be with me to the bottom of the page,
Insisting on what history exacts.
Be memory, be conscience, will and rage,
And keep me cold and honest, cousin coat,
So if I lie, I'll know you're at my throat.

The Yard

White overflow, white wall.
The frosted window, framed in black.
A plantpot long abandoned by the classics.
All the other sleepers here
Who made this doorless yard their own,
A vacancy where fiction writes
It memoranda to the world.
No ins, no outs, but here we are.
The Belgian sensualist Van Loup
Abandoned wit as well as sin
To embark on his journal of light.
He would climb from this window
To crouch with a campstool,
Awaiting ten minutes a day
When the yard was engaged by the sun,
And then watch as his shadow
Was formed and absorbed by the wall.
Veronique, who sang and danced,
Was aware of the yard in her mirror
But mainly concerned with how best
To fit wardrobes enough in the room
To conceal all her lovers at once
From each other, and pondering this
She failed to see the murderer,
Attired as an acrobat, step down
Inside the yard and don his gloves.
Group Captain Flack conceived the walls
As a chamber in nimbus. Awaiting Von Zundert
The Camel could circle, secure
In a gin-engined terror, forever.
And others are only disclosed
By the rustle of visiting cards,
But the distance that cancels their voices
Can never dispose of their absence.
They never ate, or washed, or loved
Or read, or were ruined, or kissed
Or killed, in private or by process of the state,
But all of them offer the relevant postcards
Of cities where none of this happened.

They show you cathedrals, casinos and brothels,
The fleet still at anchor, the news
And the hemlines arrested, industrial ghettoes
And graveyards according to station,
Cuisine and critique and the way to bribe policemen,
The jails and the libraries, barracks
And monasteries, map-rooms, asylums,
The price of their pleasure and how it was paid.
What you hear is these people insisting –
Not written in Latin or Teuton,
Not written in Volapuk, algebra,
Enzyme or semaphore, braille, blood or code,
But in breath on the windows of trains,
In invisible ink on your lover's back,
All from the viewpoint of Proteus
Now, in a language that does not exist,
In the tongue the yard speaks
To the living, the dead, and all those
Who are neither but cry to be heard.

Fiction and the Reading Public

You read, and then you go to sleep:
That's work's permission to be dead.
And while you sleep you watch them pulp
Whole libraries you have not read.

They make you read what money writes,
A thing left in a carriage,
Spine unbroken, loud with secrets,
Fifty Ways to Wreck Your Marriage . . .

Dexter had to give up reading –
Lulu said it wasted time
When he could give himself to money.
Dexter planned the perfect crime.

Dexter stunned her with a bundle
Of old *Partisan Reviews*.
The arm discovered in Death Valley
Livened up the evening news.

If Lulu stands for capital
And Dexter stands for wit,
If Lulu's in the mortuary
And Dexter's deep in shit,

Then what's required is a book –
Psychosis in a Trailer!
Someone put the money up
And sent for Norman Mailer.

Mailer worked on it for hours.
The plans he made were vast,
And though in fact no text appeared
He spent the money fast.

When Dex said, Norm, I'd love to read
My life before I vanish,
Mailer shrugged, I'm sorry, Dex,
I just can't seem to finish:

My novel need not terminate
Because its hero fries.
Remember, fiction's *fictional*,
And therefore never dies.

When Dexter hung his head and cried,
But Norman, wait a minute:
What kind of story stays alive
Without the hero in it?

Mailer punched the grille and said,
You've got me beaten, Jack.
Go shoot the Pope. Read Wittgenstein.
But just get off my back.

Of that of which I cannot speak
I am condemned to silence,
Plus *you're* condemned, let's not forget,
For readership with violence.

As Mailer left, he did not mourn
The book he had not made:
He only muttered to a guard
That art had been betrayed.

They came to Dexter on Death Row
And asked his final need,
And Dexter said, I don't suppose
There's anything to read?

They brought him *Fonda's Workout Book*
And *How to be a Sucker*.
Here Dex, these ought to shut you up,
Pretentious little fucker.

Poem of the Decadence

Cancelled passions. Bills unpaid and mail
In pigeonholes, then in the hands of clerks,
Then sent somewhere and on return
At long last put to death
In the enormous warehouse with the chimney.
Hence the yellow afternoons
The town endures with such bad grace,
In one of which I'm writing you
This letter, which I recommence
Each day at just this point.

Whatever's not been sold or thieved –
Their underwear, their own long-unsent mail,
The suits in which they stand, their names –
They gather up and try to leave
In a last reassertion of innocence, hoping
To step on the ferry, cross over and simply get off
And be changed and have something to do.
Then it's only a lake, and back they come
With a will to disguise their resentment
And press on with being themselves.

But the quayside is littered with napkins
They've clenched unawares and then dropped
At the sight of policemen
Too daft or too good at their jobs to believe
Any suspect's been out and has simply 'come back,
As you do' – they believe in the rules
In the book no one else ever sees,
Which appear to derive from a mixture
Of cruel common sense and wild fancy
Distilled from a torturer's journal.

Doomed, distracted, the victims look round
And the ferry is already gone,
Looking foreign and wholly convincing
And leaving the scum to resettle
Around the tall props of the pier
Where it seems they'll be spending the evening

Neck-deep and in chains among refuse
While river-policemen come by in their punts
To gain updates by moonlight, all shaking their heads,
Which is as it should be, I'm assured.

At dead of night the warehouse furnace burns
As urgently as ever,
Dictating its letters of smoke to the stars.
The fishermen slip with their catch on long poles
Through unlit streets to scale the roof.
Of an average midnight a dozen or more
Can be found there with liquor,
Their lines lowered into the chimney.
They've no other role but to parody us
With their simple attachment to money and pleasure:
By dawn they have all disappeared.

It is then I must have the fine detail:
The quivering eyes of the sud on the shoreline
That lingers to regrease the stones:
Across the lake a flapping line of sheets
That has never delivered a message:
The roar underfoot and fine torrential ash
As if fire redoubled its fury:
A scream that is waiting and waiting
But never delivered, set in a throat
Like an attitude soon to be scorned.
So it's time to confess, but to what?
If I thought it would help
I would even explain I've been wounded in love
And deserve it because I've been bad,
Repeatedly, with relish, though I could not now
Assert with confidence exactly who
Is giving me this pain. Or else
Is waiting punishment itself?

Despite this last I've grown convinced
The personal does not exist.
And yet in finishing I'm bound to ask
On looking out across the roofs
And seeing that column still rising,
And blurring the city with phonemes of ash,

Then what is burning really? Who's it for?
Or is it simply one more rule?
And in framing these questions I've learned
I must try a departure myself,
And even supposing you know what the answers might be
Or are even convinced they exist,
You will not have the pleasure of telling me now,
For I called this the town of dead letters
And this one is mine. Let it burn.

Tonight

The light leaves too slowly
For us to regret it.
The birds, as they pin out
Their musical maps
On the blue and gold air,
Make England respectable, almost.

The back doors stand open,
Inviting the summer.
Some people are reading at windows
And others in couples
Stand talking in gardens, amazed
To discover they've already met.

Like guests who have given up waiting
We find ourselves at home
Amid this uninspected calm
Too large to call an accident
Or any use to man or beast,
Except, tonight, for living in.

A Matinee

The shops, the banks, the bars are shut.
The square smells like a cinema,
All breath and chocolate and sweat.

The islands' washed-out distance
Means the fifties' rotten movies
Where I learned how to be bored

With love and money on location,
Postcard Europes, plots I couldn't grasp.
The starlets in their wide white skirts

Were always speeding on the cliffs
Or flinging into rooms to weep
At letters or the lack of them,

While stationed in the cypresses
Their leading men would smoke and stare
At nightfall, as the orchestra

Cranked up its fatuous claims
That the issue was passion,
Which seemed even worse than the adverts.

The stylists of never and nowhere
With nothing to do but rehearse
To the vacant plush darkness

And me with my headache and choc-ice.
Tedious wealth, I sympathised.
So when today I'm dull enough

To be Rossano Brazzi, let me sing,
Desert you, loom in archways, ask
About the past or unctuously show you

How the fishermen eat fish, then pose
Beside the ocean, signifying grief.
White girls in white skirts

With invisible legs and no sex,
Sealed in your villas being old,
Since all that I can manage is

To run those afternoons again,
I've left my number at the desk:
What better offers are there now?

In the Fifties

When I wiped the snow clear
The pond in the flints was a pane of smoked ice
Where I had no reflection,
A sky-coloured, no coloured
Mind-your-own-business. I liked it.
The flakes went on falling.
They covered my hand where it rested.
The sky was dissolving
On hedges and lintels,
Expanding our town to a state of Alaska,
Slap in the notional middle of nowhere.
I thought of snow mounting the staircase,
Absorbing the bath, reproducing
The pillows and sheets, and then masking the faces
That lay and accepted the Ice Age
As if it were air, or the passage of time.
In that general effacement I waited for mine.

In Madre Maria
(for George Charlton)

The priest and the police chief are in the back room.
They consider elections, the drought and the war.
When their glasses are smashed they are deaf to the boom.
There are more in the cellar. It's happened before.

Since Marquez, men say, there is nothing unique.
There is no one to witness what no longer boggles.
The runway is short. The pigs do not speak.
But soon, as one pig, they will put on their goggles.

Kingdom of Kiev, Rios das Muertes

All afternoon, the streets are deaf with snow,
Its dripping dud piano muted,
The fire in the garden silently burning,
The visitors visiting others. Midwinter.
Words grow from each other to conquer the board
With childhood's careful mania.
The Kingdom of Kiev is colder than Hell
And Los Rios das Muertes are many –
Lies concerning geography,
The inexhaustible resource
From the era of General Knowledge,
Where Tupper and Wilson still circle the track
And an amateur Norwegian goalie
Whose name I'm afraid I've forgotten
Has kept a clean sheet for three years.
Consider the baking of salmon
In riverbank mud, and the means of ensuring
That wells dug in marshland run clear,
The feathers, the lead, how high the moon
And what precisely Grant had drunk
At Appomatox – useful stuff,
Assuming six times six will still
Fend off the nuns and chewing-gum
Enfolds the heart, and the air-bubble
Trapped in the co-pilot's molar explodes
At twenty thousand over Skaggerat . . .
If the Kingdom of Kiev is colder than Hell
Take furs to exchange and be careful
To sip the right side of the fiery bowl,
Not forgetting the boxes of Dickens.
If Los Rios das Muertes are many,
Choose one and remember your journal:
Observe how it breaks into leaf.
Slip a hand in the wet-velvet blackness
By night, in the squamous dun khaki by day.
Honour your dad on his moped,
Come home bearing gifts from the blizzard –
In Muscovy, The Fawcett Expedition,
Marrying tundra and tropic

As suitable places for anyone versed
In the pointless collection of facts.
The telephone won't ring, but if it does
I'll know until I pick it up
That the atlas has finally called.

The Head Man
(for Margoulis Grolsz)

You say you've been back for a look.
You're struck by the impressive podium,
The throne in which the Head Man sat
And ground his teeth with gout,
Dispensing justice and the lash
To the 'conference of funeral directors'
Who listened in pustular torpor
From the Main Hall's fog of breakfast farts
To the news that we could not speak English
Or read it, and ought to avoid it,
And worst of all ate in the street
Without caps on. Ah yes,
I remember it well, being frightened and wrong
On a permanent basis, secure
In the knowledge you'd never be short of a row,
And the lesson remains,
In this world of strong women
Who put me in mind of that pantomime demon
Revolving the dice in his head to decide
If today was for charm or for excoriation.
I stuck to my books, but my verses were proof
That the Russians had sent me
To fire the Hall, rape Edna the typist,
Abstract the school fund and be famous
And not know the value of money.
In fact all I stole was a copy
Of *Culture and Anarchy*. Touchstone, indeed:
It retains its original boredom,
Safe and stale in custard covers.
I read it last night when you'd rung,
Fell asleep and then dreamed of the journey
We'd talked our way out of for years –
By Araguaya, Negro and Las Muertes
To the utmost Amazonas, by canoe,
Our only plan: escape the map!
In the feverish heaven of jiggers,
Long after the final dry sock and the whisky,
Sick of mandioca, sick of fish,

Where the river runs into the sky and the trees
Form an endless and foetid arcade
With the promise of nothing beyond it – lost,
With the whole undertaking distinctly
Like something in Conrad gone wrong,
We arrived in the clearing, in which stood the hut
With its trellis of head-sporting poles.
When we ventured inside he was there,
Drinking port from a skull, reading Arnold
And saying, 'Late again. Explain yourselves.'

Geography
(for Gerry)

Tonight the blue that's flowing in
Beneath the window gloves my hands
With coolness, as indifferent as a nurse.
The ridge of forest wears grey smoke
Against grey pink, then deeper blue
Discloses what I cannot see,
The channel's distant bays, their sands
Drawn into shape by bows of surf,
Then further capes and promontories,
Sea-pines and isthmuses and island stepping
Out from island, all
Remoter than a name can reach.
Out there is home, a hammered strand
By some unvisitable sea,
Beyond all empire and all sense,
Enduring minus gender, case and tense,
A landfall, past imagining and free.